THE ECCENTRIC'S QUOTATION BOOK

The Eccentric's Quotation Book

A Literary Companion

Edited by
SIMON PETHERICK

ROBERT HALE · LONDON

Preface and selection © Simon Petherick 1994
First published in Great Britain 1994

ISBN 0 7090 5398 3

Robert Hale Limited
Clerkenwell House
Clerkenwell Green
London EC1R 0HT

2   4   6   8   10   9   7   5   3   1

Photoset in Goudy by
Derek Doyle & Associates, Mold, Clwyd.
Printed and bound in Great Britain by
WBC Ltd, Bridgend, Mid-Glamorgan

Preface

Eccentrics are odd. As Lytton Strachey so memorably described them, they perform 'a strange meteoric course'. They are people for whom common conventions and accepted modes of behaviour are not so much flouted as totally unrecognized.

There are not many people who do not feel some tenderness for eccentricity. Most of us would probably be happy to be so unaware of how out of step with the rest of mankind our behaviour was. Even those who act as the guardians of our laws and constitutions can often see the value of the eccentric – as a US Supreme Court Justice, William O. Douglas, said, 'I do not know of any salvation for society except through eccentrics.'

At the same time, not many of us would be quite so happy to be so close to eccentricity for long. You would not want to rely on an eccentric to perform a delicate surgical operation, and you might be doubtful whether a train service run by eccentrics would ever get you to your destination on time.

It is comforting to know that eccentrics exist, because as long as they do then we do not have to behave eccentrically ourselves. There is a poignancy to many of the quotations in this book, a hint of the loneliness which the eccentric, with all his absurd fixations and obsessions, is destined to know.

Many of the writers collected here attempt to saddle eccentricity to some view about society as a whole. British politicians are often keen to point to the deep strain of eccentricity in British life as an example of the freedoms available in that country; a Spaniard, however, would identify the tales of Don Quixote as those of a man for whom freedoms are irrelevant compared to his own sense of pride.

Whatever the reason behind eccentricity, the quotations in this book show that above all, eccentrics can make us laugh. For that alone, we should be grateful to them.

Acknowledgements

I am grateful to the following for permission to quote from works in copyright: *Adolf Hitler: My Part in his Downfall* by Spike Milligan, Michael Joseph Ltd; *All About Ourselves and Other Essays* by J.B. Priestley, Peters Fraser and Dunlop; *The English Eccentrics* by Edith Sitwell, Faber and Faber; *The Most of S.J. Perelman* by S.J. Perelman, Peters Fraser and Dunlop; *I Wonder What Happened to Him?* by Noel Coward, Michael Imison Playwrights Ltd; *The Eccentric Life of Alexander Cruden* by Edith Oliver, Faber and Faber; *The Naked Civil Servant* by Quentin Crisp, Jonathan Cape; *The Natives Are Restless* by Idries Shah, Octagon Press Ltd; *The Abortion* by Richard Brautigan, Jonathan Cape; *W.H. Auden: The Life of A Poet* by Charles Osborne, Penguin Books Ltd; *If the War Goes On* by Hermann Hesse, Suhrkamp Verlag; *The Book of Heroic Failures* by Stephen Pile, Routledge and Kegan Paul. Every attempt has been made to seek copyright permissions, but any omissions will be remedied in future editions of this book.

Why must I be accounted rebellious, undutiful, because I cannot see as you see, and think as you think?

SUSAN EDMONSTONE FERRIER (1782–1854)
The Inheritance
1824

Coleridge holds that a man cannot have a pure mind who refuses apple-dumplings. I am not certain but he is right.

CHARLES LAMB (1775–1834)
Essays of Elia: 'Grace Before Meat'

The biographies of men who have essentially differed from the rest of the human race, either by their having been born with some peculiar congenital defect, or possessing an eccentricity of character, which inevitably impels them to overlap and trespass from the boundaries of the beaten highway of conventional life, have been in all times eagerly sought after by the curious enquirer into human nature.

HENRY WILSON AND JAMES CAULFIELD
The Book of Wonderful Characters
1869

Here give me some Sack.
Says old Tun-belly'd Jack.

Deviation from common rules, when they proceed from genius, are not merely pardonable, but admirable.

> FANNY BURNEY (1752–1840)
> *Cecilia*
> 1782

Lady Hester is not mad. Madness which is written so strongly in the eyes is not expressed in her beautiful and amiable look. Folly, which always betrays itself in conversation, interrupting the sequence by irregular, eccentric and sudden departures from the subject is in no way to be perceived in the elevated, mystic and cloudy, but well–sustained and connected conversation of her Ladyship.

> ALPHONSE DE LAMARTINE (1790–1869) on LADY
> HESTER STANHOPE (1776–1839), traveller
> in *Souvenirs de l'Orient*
> 1835

Eccentricity has always abounded when and where strength of character has abounded, and the amount of eccentricity in a society has generally been proportional to the amount of genius, mental vigour, and moral courage it contained. That so few now dare to be eccentric marks the chief danger of the time.

> J. S. MILL (1806–73)
> *On Liberty*
> 1859

John Christie, the rich and enterprising founder of the Glyndebourne Festival Opera, was not above using his distinguished position to indulge a schoolboy sense of fun. Sitting next to the Queen at dinner one evening, he removed his glass eye and polished it for several minutes with his handkerchief. When he had finished, he popped it back, turned to the Queen and asked 'In straight, Ma'am?'

    CATHERINE CAUFIELD
    The Emperor of the United States of America and
    other Magnificent British Eccentrics
    1981

To the most famous, infamous, high and mighty Feeder, Nicholas Wood, Great and Grand Gormandizer of Harrisom, in the County of Kent: Most exorbitant Paunchmonger, I having taken much unnecessary paines in writing these few collections of your deserving Acts, in memory thereof have erected this Monument of incke and paper. Herostratus was famous for burning the Temple of Diana in Ephesus: Dedalus for flying in the Ayre, and Leander for swimming over the Hellespontinck sea. So by this small Treatise of your vertues with your unmatchable exploits be preserved to posterity, that time or oblivion shall never eate out or devoure the happy memory of your eating.

> preface to JOHN TAYLOR (1578–1653)
> *The Great Eater of Kent, or part of the admirable Teeth and Stomacks Exploits of Nicholas Wood*
> 1630

Our attitude's queer and quaint;
You're wrong if you think it ain't.

> SIR W. S. GILBERT (1836–1911)
> *The Mikado*
> 1885

In truth he was a strange and wayward wight,
Fond of each gentle, and each dreadful scene.
In darkness and in storm he found delight.

> JAMES BEATTIE (1735–1803)
> *The Minstrel*
> 1771

If God delights so much in variety, as all things animate and inanimate sufficiently prove, no wonder that man should do so too: and I have now been so accustomed to move, though slowly, that I intend to creep on to my journey's end, by which means I may live to have been an inhabitant of every town almost in Europe, and die as I have lately (and wish I had always) lived, a free citizen of the whole world, slave to no sect nor subject to any king.

> CAPTAIN PHILIP THICKNESSE (1719–92)
> *Memoirs and Anecdotes*
> 1788

'How pleasant to know Mr Lear!'
Who has written such volumes of stuff!
Some think him ill-tempered and queer,
But a few think him pleasant enough.

> EDWARD LEAR (1812–88)
> preface to *Nonsense Songs*
> 1871

Oh! he is mad, is he? Then I wish he would bite some other of my generals.

> KING GEORGE II (1683–1760)
> on General James Wolfe (1727–59)

'There's been an accident!' they said,
'Your servant's cut in half; he's dead!'
'Indeed!' said Mr Jones, 'and please,
Send me the half that's got my keys.'

> HARRY GRAHAM (1874–1936)
> *Ruthless Rhymes for Heartless Homes:* 'Mr Jones'

GEORGE PRINCE of WALES.
born 12 August 1762.

Whenever I watch how a man behaves when he is alone, I always conclude that he is insane – I can find no other word for it. I first noticed this when I was still a boy: a clown named Rondale, an Englishman, who was walking along the dark and deserted passages of a circus, took off his top hat to a mirror and bowed respectfully to his own reflection. There was no one in the passage but himself. I was sitting on a cistern over his head and so was invisible to him, and had thrust out my head just at the moment when he made his respectful bow. This action of the clown plunged me into dark and unpleasant speculations. He was a clown, and what is more, an Englishman, whose profession – or art – lay in his eccentricity.

MAXIM GORKY (1868–1936)
Fragments From My Diary

I wish I loved the Human Race;
I wish I loved its silly face;
I wish I liked the way it walks;
I wish I liked the way it talks;
And when I'm introduced to one
I wish I thought *What Jolly Fun!*

SIR WALTER ALEXANDER RALEIGH (1861–1922)
Laughter From a Cloud

If individuality has no play, society does not advance; if individuality breaks out of all bounds, society perishes.

    THOMAS HENRY HUXLEY (1825–95)
    Administrative Nihilism
    1871

One day [William Pitt] asked Newcastle to come to his house to discuss plans. The duke found him ill in bed in a cold room. Pitt had much to say, and the duke found the cold unbearable; at last, spying another bed in the room, he crept into it, and the two statesmen were found talking and gesticulating at one another from under the bed-clothes.

    BASIL WILLIAMS
    William Pitt, Earl of Chatham
    1913

'My address,' said Mr Micawber, 'is Windsor Terrace, City Road. I – in short,' said Mr Micawber, with the same genteel air, and in another burst of confidence – 'I live there.'

I made him a bow.

'Under the impression,' said Mr Micawber, 'that your peregrinations in this metropolis have not as yet been extensive, and that you might have some difficulty in penetrating the arcana of the Modern Babylon in the direction of the City Road, – in short,' said Mr Micawber, in another burst of confidence,

'that you might lose yourself – I shall be happy to call
this evening, and install you in the knowledge of the
nearest way.'

I thanked him with all my heart, for it was friendly
in him to offer to take that trouble.

> CHARLES DICKENS (1812–70)
> *The History of David Copperfield*
> 1849

'You are old, Father William,' the young man said,
'And your hair has become very white;
And yet you incessantly stand on your head –
Do you think, at your age, it is right?'

'In my youth,' Father William replied to his son,
'I feared it might injure the brain;
But now that I'm perfectly sure I have none,
Why I do it again and again.'

> LEWIS CARROLL (1832–98)
> *Alice's Adventures in Wonderland*
> 1865

England is the paradise of individuality, eccentricity,
heresy, anomalies, hobbies, and humours.

> GEORGE SANTAYANA (1863–1952)
> *Soliloquies in England:* 'The British Character'
> 1922

It is impossible to say what will suit eccentric persons.
  GEORGE ELIOT (1819–80)
  Middlemarch
  1871

The earliest record of Henry [Bradley, 1845–1923] is singularly characteristic. It was before he was four years old, on the occasion of his being taken for the first time to church where he obstinately persisted in holding his book upside-down. This eccentricity gave [his parents] some anxiety, until it was discovered that the child really could read, but only with the book in that position. Unbeknown to them he had taught himself during family prayers: while his father, sitting with a great Bible open on his knees, was reading the lesson aloud, the boy, standing in front of him closely poring over the page, had followed word by word and thus worked out the whole puzzle – and so completely, that long after he had accustomed himself to the normal position he could read equally well either way.
  ROBERT BRIDGES (1844–1930)
  Three Friends
  1932

Sir Francis Dashwood (1708–81) could pass from unholy orgies at Medmenham to serious discussions on art and archeology; he could divide his money and his time between the impious parodying of religious rites and those schemes which helped to do so much for the art culture in this country; he could leave the attractions of women and wine to stand up for a man who was being hounded to death for an idea ... [he] was a rake, but he was not all bad.

> E. BERESFORD CHANCELLOR
> *The Lives of the Rakes*, Vol. IV
> 1925

I don't mind where people make love, so long as they don't do it in the street and frighten the horses.

> MRS PATRICK CAMPBELL (1865–1940)
> alleged

Lord Ronald said nothing; he flung himself from the room, flung himself upon his horse, and rode madly off in all directions.

> STEPHEN BUTLER LEACOCK (1869–1944)
> *Nonsense Novels:* 'Gertrude the Governess'
> 1911

To survive you must have a strong brain, an assertive ego, a dynamic character. In your luncheon-parties, in old days, the remains of the guests were taken away with the debris of the feast. I have often lunched with you in Park Lane and found myself the only survivor.

> OSCAR WILDE (1854–1900)
> letter to Frank Harris (1856–1931), 1897

For, by the laws of Spirit, in the right
Is every individual character
That acts in strict consistency with itself.
Self-contradiction is the only wrong.
> JOHANN CHRISTOPH FRIEDRICH VON SCHILLER
> (1759–1805)
> *Wallenstein's Tod*

Not long after their marriage Mr and Mrs Lytton Bulwer ... were travelling in an open carriage along the Riviera, between Genoa and Spezzia; Lord Lytton was dressed in the somewhat fantastic costume which

at that period he affected … Passing through one of
the many villages close to the sea, they observed a
singularly handsome girl standing at a cottage door.
Mr Bulwer, with somewhat ill-advised complacency,
said, 'Did you notice how that girl looked at me?' The
lady replied, 'The girl was not looking at you in
admiration; if you wear that ridiculous dress, no
wonder people stare at you.' The bridegroom … said,
'You think that people stare at my dress; and not at
me: I will give you the most absolute and convincing
proof that your theory has no foundation.' He then
proceeded to divest himself of every particle of
clothing except his hat and boots: and taking the
place of the lady's maid, drove for ten miles in this
normal condition.

SIR WILLIAM FRASER
Hic et Ubique
1893

In a bowl to sea went wise men three,
On a brilliant night in June.
They carried a net, and their hearts were set
On fishing up the moon.

THOMAS LOVE PEACOCK (1785–1866)
The Wise Men of Gotham
1837

I am like an unpopular electric eel in a pond full of flatfish.

> EDITH SITWELL (1887–1964)
> quoted in *A Nest of Tigers* by John Lehmann,
> 1969

The worst actor ever to appear on a stage anywhere was Robert 'Romeo' Coates (1772–1842) ... His total incapacity to play any part whatever, combined with his insistence upon wearing diamonds from head to foot, regardless of role, and his tendency to 'improve' upon Shakespeare as he went along, made him immensely popular with astonished audiences up and down Britain.

> STEPHEN PILE
> *The Book of Heroic Failures*
> 1979

Restraint from ill is freedom to the wise;
But Englishmen do all restraint despise.

> DANIEL DEFOE (1659–1731)
> *The True-Born Englishman*
> 1701

More cranks take up unfashionable error than unfashionable truths.

> BERTRAND RUSSELL (1872–1970)
> *Unpopular Essays: An Outline of Intellectual Rubbish*
> 1950

Jack Adams, Professor of the Celestial Sciences of Clerkenwell Green, was a blind buzzard, who pretended to have the eyes of an eagle. He was chiefly employed in horary questions, relative to love and marriage; and knew, upon proper occasions, how to soothe and flatter the expectations of those who consulted him, as a man might have much better fortune from him for five guineas than for the same number of shillings. He affected a singular dress and cast horoscopes with great solemnity. When he failed in his predictions, he declared that the stars did not actually force, but powerfully incline, and threw the blame on wayward and perverse fate.

> GRANGER'S *BIOGRAPHICAL DICTIONARY*
> on Jack Adams (1625– ?), astrologer and
> conjuror

> Snowy, Flowy, Blowy,
> Showery, Flowery, Bowery,
> Hoppy, Croppy, Droppy,
> Breezy, Sneezy, Freezy.
> SIR GREGORY GANDER (1745–1815)
> *The Twelve Months*

A man far oftener appears to have a decided character from persistently following his temperament than from persistently following his principles.

> FRIEDRICH WILHELM NIETZSCHE (1844–1900)
> *Human, All Too Human*

Ann Moore ... about the beginning of 1807 ... first excited the public attention by declaring she could live without food ... In order to satisfy the public, she was removed from her home to the house of Mr. Jackson, grocer, of the same village, and all the inhabitants were invited to join in watching her ... which continued sixteen days ... This juggler was committed to prison in February 1816, for falsely collecting money under the pretence of charity.

> HENRY WILSON AND JAMES CAULFIELD
> *The Book of Wonderful Characters*
> 1869

All poets are mad.

> ROBERT BURTON (1577–1640)
> Anatomy of Melancholy

I hate the common herd of men and keep them afar. Let there be sacred silence: I, the Muses' priest, sing for girls and boys songs not heard before.

> HORACE (65–8 BC)
> *Odes*
> 23 BC

Robert, alias 'Linen' Cooke, of Cappoquin ... was a very eccentric and wealthy gentleman, and had several estates in both England and Ireland ... Amongst other peculiarities he had his coach drawn by white horses, and their harness made of hemp and linen. His cows were also white ... From his constantly wearing none but linen garments, and using linen generally for other purposes, he acquired the appellation, 'Linen Cooke'.

> J. BERNARD BURKE
> Anecdotes of the Aristocracy
> 1849

For Allah created the English mad – the maddest of all mankind.

> RUDYARD KIPLING (1865–1936)
> Kitchener's School

He had great taste, which had been cultivated by foreign travel, and having an ample fortune, he was able to indulge in many whims and caprices, by which some were led to doubt of his sanity; but others who judged him better ascribed them to the self-indulgence of a man out of harmony with his time and contemptuously indifferent to what the world might say of him.

> CHARLES LEVER (1806–72)
> *The Bramleighs of Bishop's Folly*
> 1833
> the character described was based on the Early
> Bishop of Derry, 1730–1803

At the pre-emptory request and desire of a large majority of the citizens of the United States, I, Joshua A. Norton, declare and proclaim myself Emperor of the United States and in virtue of the authority thereby in me vested, do hereby order and direct the representatives of the different states of the Union to assemble in Musical Hall, of this city, on the last day of February next, then and there to make such alteration in the existing laws of the Union as may ameliorate the evils under which the country is laboring and thereby cause confidence to exist, both at home and abroad, in our stability and integrity.

> NORTON I (1819–80), Emperor of the United States
> as printed in the *San Francisco Bulletin*, 17 October 1859
> Norton assumed the title of Emperor of the United States and Protector of Mexico for twenty years

Great chieftain o' the pudding-race.
> ROBERT BURNS (1759–96)
> *Address to a Haggis*

I am a true thinker and speaker. I cannot stand or endure the priggery, caddery, snobbery, smuggery, hypocrisy, lies, flattery, compliments, praise, jealousy, envy, pretence, conventional speech and behaviour and affected artificial behaviour upon which society is based.

> BEATRICE MILES (1902–73), Australian eccentric
> quoted in *Ratbags* by Keith Dunstan, 1979

I once ate a pea.
>BEAU BRUMMELL (1778–1840)
>on being asked at dinner whether he ever ate
>vegetables
>quoted in *Familiar Short Sayings of Great Men* by
>SAMUEL A. BENT, 1887

I left my carriage yesterday evening on the way to town from the Pavilion, and the infidel of a landlord put me into a room with a damp stranger.
>BEAU BRUMMELL (1778–1840)
>on being asked why he had such a bad cold
>Ibid.

'Have some wine,' the March Hare said in an encouraging tone. Alice looked all round the table, but there was nothing on it but tea. 'I don't see any wine,' she remarked. 'There isn't any,' said the March Hare.
>LEWIS CARROLL (1832–98)
>*Alice's Adventures in Wonderland*
>1865

There has always been a strong strain of extravagance in the governing families of England; from time to time they throw off some peculiarly ill-balanced member, who performs a strange meteoric course.
>LYTTON STRACHEY (1880–1932)
>in *The Athenaeum*, 4 April 1919

THE MARCH HARE.

I do not know of any salvation for society except through eccentrics, misfits, dissenters, people who protest.

> WILLIAM O. DOUGLAS (1898–1980), US Supreme Court Justice
> quoted in *The Power of Reason* by Robert M. Hutchins, 1964

Sitting one day among a company, mostly of the fair sex, at Lady Onslow's, a large fly which had buzzed about him a long time, at last settled upon the bonnet of one of the ladies, which the doctor (The Reverend George Harvest) observing, got up, and with a grave look and acccent, addressed these words aloud to the fly, 'May you be married!' and watching his opportunity to kill it, he lifted his hand, and gave the lady such a blow upon the head as quite deranged her attire.

HENRY WILSON
The Eccentric Mirror
1813

People say that life is the thing, but I prefer reading.

LOGAN PEARSALL SMITH (1865–1946)
Afterthoughts: 'Myself'
1931

And the sun sank again on the grand Australian bush – the nurse and tutor of eccentric minds, the home of the weird, and of much that is different from things in other lands.

HENRY HERTZBERG LAWSON (1867–1922)
Rats

I am pleased to believe that beauty is at bottom incompatible with ill, and therefore am so eccentric as to have confidence in the latent benignity of that beautiful creature, the rattlesnake, whose lithe neck and burnished maze of tawny gold, as he sleekly curls aloft in the sun, who on the prairie can behold without wonder?

HERMAN MELVILLE (1819–91)
The Confidence-Man: His Masquerade
1857

He had been eight years upon a project for extracting sunbeams out of cucumbers, which were to be put in phials hermetically sealed, and let out to warm the air in raw, inclement summers.

JONATHAN SWIFT (1667–1745)
Gulliver's Travels
1726

The pitiful prevalence of general conformity extirpates genius and murders originality.

FANNY BURNEY (1752–1840)
Cecilia
1782

My father, gifted though he was, spent his life apart, alone. Indelibly stained with gothic darkness and its accompanying colours, pure and soft in tone, his mind inhabited that ivory tower of the thirteenth

century, complete with every convenience of the time
– cross-bows, battlements, oubliettes and
thumbscrews – that growing unhappiness had obliged
him to construct for his protection against the
exterior and contemporary world.

OSBERT SITWELL (1892–1969)
Left Hand, Right Hand!
1945

I am reborn. I am born from the egg. It is a perfect
cube.

SALVADOR DALI (1904–1989)
as he stepped out of a large white egg in the
middle of Rome

So she went into the garden to cut a cabbage-leaf, to
make an apple pie; and at the same time a great
she-bear, coming up the street, pops its head into the
shop. 'What! no soap?' So he died, and she very
imprudently married the barber; and there were
present the Picininnies, and the Joblillies, and the
Garyalies, and the grand Panjandrum himself, with
the little round button at top, and they all fell to
playing the game of catch as catch can till the gun
powder ran out at the heels of their boots.

SAMUEL FOOTE (1720–77)
in *Harry and Lucy Concluded* by Maria
Edgeworth (1767–1849)

I never hated a man enough to give him his diamonds back.

ZSA ZSA GABOR
quoted in *The Observer*, 28 August 1957

On looking at myself in the mirror I can see at once that my face is anything but comely. Continual exposure to the sun and the rains of the tropics has furrowed it in places and given it a tint which neither Rowland's Kalydor, nor all the cosmetics on Belinda's toilette, would ever be able to remove.

CHARLES WINTERTON (1782–1865)
Essays on Natural History

The doctor [William Butler, 1535–1618] was lying at the Savoy in London, where was a balcony looked into the Thames, a patient came to him that was grievously tormented with the ague. The doctor orders a boat to be in readiness under his window, and discoursed with the patient (a gentleman) in the balcony, when on a signal given, two or three lusty fellows came behind the gentleman and threw him a matter of 20 feet into the Thames. This surprise absolutely cured him.

JOHN AUBREY (1626–97)
Brief Lives
this was one of many eccentric cures practised by Doctor Butler, according to Aubrey

You must not mind me, Madam; I say strange things, but I mean no harm.

> SAMUEL JOHNSON (1709–84)
> remark to Fanny Burney (1752–1840), quoted in her diary, 23 August 1778

He did everything in his own odd and eccentric way. Being one day roused by a strange shouting I went out and discovered it was Manning who, wishing to cross the water and finding no-one who would attend to him, commenced a series of howls like a dog supplemented by execrations derived from the Chinese vernacular. This led our attendant Mandarins to infer that he had gone mad, and they lost no time in conveying him over the river – which was all he wanted.

> SIR JOHN DAVIS, interpreter
> on THOMAS MANNING (1772–1840), doctor and traveller in Tibet
> quoted in *Eccentric Travellers* by John Keay, 1982

She is one of those geniuses who find some diabolical enjoyment in being dreaded and detested by their fellow-creatures.

> TOBIAS GEORGE SMOLLETT (1721–71)
> *The Expedition of Humphry Clinker*
> 1771

[Would Lord Byron] take soup? 'No; he never took soup.' – Would he take some fish? 'No; he never took fish.' – Presently I asked if he would eat some mutton. 'No; he never ate mutton.' – I then asked if he would take a glass of wine. 'No; he never tasted wine.' – It was now necessary to enquire what he *did* eat and drink; and the answer was 'Nothing but hard biscuits and soda-water.' Unfortunately, neither hard biscuits nor soda-water were at hand; and he dined upon potatoes bruised down on his plate and drenched with vinegar ... Some days after, meeting Hobhouse, I said to him, 'How long will Lord Byron persevere in his present diet?' He replied: 'Just as long as you continue to notice it.'

SAMUEL ROGERS (1763–1855)
The Table-Talk of Samuel Rogers

I advocate Free Love in its highest, purest sense, as the only cure for the immorality, the deep damnation by which men corrupt and disfigure God's most holy institution of sexual relations.

VICTORIA WOODHULL (1838–1927)
in an advertisement in the *New York Times* in 1870, announcing her intention to run for President

Some deemed him wondrous wise, and some believed him mad.

> JAMES BEATTIE (1735–1803)
> *The Minstrel*
> 1771

A woman is only a woman, but a good Cigar is a Smoke.

> RUDYARD KIPLING (1865–1936)
> *The Betrothed*

Very brilliant, very clever, very courageous, self-controlled and self-reliant, boldly contemptuous of society and social conventionalities – but with no secret spring of love and tenderness in that cold and indifferent heart.

> W.H. DAVENPORT ADAMS
> Child-Life and Girlhood of Remarkable Women
> 1892
> describing Lady Mary Wortley Montagu (1690–1762)

Each the known track of sage philosophy
Deserts, and has a byway of his own;
So much the restless eagerness to shine,
And love of singularity, prevail.

> DANTE ALIGHIERI (1265–1321)
> *Paradise*

A certain recluse once said that no bonds attached him to this life, and the only thing he would regret leaving was the sky.

YOSHIDA KENKO (1283–1350)
Essays in Idleness
1340

Your experience will be a lesson to all us men not to marry ladies in very high positions.

IDI AMIN, Ugandan President
in a letter to Lord Snowdon after the latter's
divorce from Princess Margaret in 1976

[From the funeral instructions of Mrs Margaret Thompson, who died in Mayfair during the early part of the 19th century]: Six men to be my bearers, who are known to be the greatest snuff-takers in the parish of St. James's, Westminster; instead of mourning, each to wear a snuff-coloured beaver hat which I desire be bought for that purpose and given to them. Six maidens of my old acquaintance, to bear my pall, each to wear a proper hood, and to carry a box filled with the best Scotch snuff to take for their refreshment as they go along.

quoted in *Great Eccentrics* by Peter Bushell, 1984

Those comfortable padded lunatic asylums which are known, euphemistically, as the stately homes of England.
> VIRGINIA WOOLF
> *The Common Reader*
> 1925

Away he went, to live in a tent;
Over in France with his regiment.
Were you there, and tell me, did you notice?
They were all out of Step but Jim.
> IRVING BERLIN (1888–1989)
> *They Were All Out Of Step But Jim*
> 1918

Even beauty cannot always palliate eccentricity.
> HONORE DE BALZAC (1799–1850)

The merit of originality is not novelty; it is sincerity. The believing man is the original man, whatsoever he believes, he believes it for himself, not for another.
> THOMAS CARLYLE (1795–1881)
> *On Heroes, Hero-Worship and the Heroic in History*
> 1841

This is a beautiful library, timed perfectly, lush and American … I 'open' the library at nine o'clock in the morning and 'close' the library at nine in the evening, but I am here twenty-four hours a day, seven days a week to receive the books. An old woman brought in a book a couple of days ago at three o'clock in the morning ... There was a heavy label pasted on the cover and written in broad green crayon across the label was the title: 'Growing Flowers By Candlelight In Hotel Rooms, by Mrs Charles Fine Adams.'

RICHARD BRAUTIGAN (1935–84)
The Abortion: An Historical Romance 1966
1970

As to his person, he was very corpulent and beastly, a mere lump of morbid flesh ... He was a fetid mass that offended his neighbours at the bar in the sharpest degree ... This hateful decay of his carcase came upon him by continual sottishness; for, to say nothing of brandy, he was seldom without a pot of ale at his nose ... He showed another qualification he had acquired, and that was to play gigs upon a harpsichord, having taught himself with the opportunity of an old virginal of his landlady's.

ROGER NORTH
Lives of the Norths
1742
on Sir Edmund Saunders (1640–83), once a penniless orphan, who rose to become Lord Chief Justice to Charles II

In the summer of 1650, a Frenchman named Floram Marchand ('The Great Water-Sprouter') was brought over from Tours to London, who professed to be able to turn water into wine, and at his vomit render not only the tincture, but the strength and smell of several wines, and several waters.

> HENRY WILSON AND JAMES CAULFIELD
> *The Book of Wonderful Characters*
> 1869

Be virtuous and you will be eccentric.

> MARK TWAIN (1835–1910)
> *Mental Photographs*

I must confess I am a fop in my heart; ill customs influence my very senses, and I have been so used to affectation that without the help of the air of the court what is natural cannot touch me.

> SIR GEORGE ETHERIDGE (1635–91)
> letter to Mr Poley, January 1688

5 September 1662: To Mr Bland's the merchant, by invitation, and among other pretty discourse, some was of Sir Jerom Bowes, Embassador from Queene Elizabeth to the Emperor of Russia – who, because some of the noblemen there would go up the stairs to the Emperor before him, he would not go up till the Emperor had ordered those two men to be dragged downstair, with their heads knocking upon every stair

till they were killed. And when he was come up, they demanded his sword of him before he entered the room; he told them, if they would have his sword, they should have his boots too; and so caused his boots to be pulled off and his nightgown and nightcap and slippers to be sent for, and made the Emperor stay till he could go in his nightdress, since he might not go as a soldier.

> SAMUEL PEPYS (1633–1703)
> *Diaries*

Life at the Taws moved in the ordinary routine of a great English household. At 7 a gong sounded for rising, at 8 a horn blew for breakfast, at 8.30 a whistle sounded for prayers, at 1 a flag was run up at half-mast for lunch, at 4 a gun was fired for afternoon tea, at 9 a first bell sounded for dressing, at 9.15 a second bell for going on dressing, while at 9.30 a rocket was sent up to indicate that dinner was ready. At midnight dinner was over, and at 1 a.m. the tolling of a bell summoned the domestics to evening prayers.

> STEPHEN BUTLER LEACOCK (1869–1944)
> *Nonsense Novels*: 'Gertrude the Governess'
> 1911

Oysters are more beautiful than any religion.

> HECTOR HUGH MUNRO, 'Saki' (1870–1916)
> *Chronicle of Clovis*
> 1911

Oyſter.

Thrippy Pilliwinx, –

Inkly tinky pobblebockle able-squabs? Flosky! Beebul trimble flosky! Okul scratch abibblebongibo, viddle squibble tog-a-tog, ferry moyassity amsky flamsky crocklefether squiggs.

Flinky wisty pomm.

Slushypipp
EDWARD LEAR (1812–88)
letter to Evelyn Baring, Lord Cromer
1850

The English are no dottier than anyone else: you can find oddness anywhere. With them, unlike other peoples, the characteristic tends to be strongly purposeful. They not only have a great pool of eccentric talent to call upon, but they make more use of it than most of us do.

IDRIES SHAH (1924–)
The Natives Are Restless
1988

Who affects useless singularities has surely a little mind.

JOHANN KASPAR LAVATER (1741–1801)

Dr Birch was very fond of angling, and devoted much time to that amusement. In order to deceive the fish, he had a dress constructed, which, when he put it on, made him appear like an old tree. His arms he conceived would appear like branches, and the line like a long spray. In this sylvan attire he used to take root by the side of a favourite stream, and imagined that his motions might seem to the fish to be the effect of the wind. He pursued this amusement for some years in the same habit, till he was ridiculed out of it by his friends.

JOHN TAYLOR (1781–1864)
Records of My Life
1832

No great genius was ever without some mixture of madness, nor can anything grand or superior to the voice of common mortals be spoken except by the agitated soul.

ARISTOTLE (384–422 BC)

PUNCH, OR THE LONDON CHARIVARI.—June 12, 1907.

THE CHAMPION FLIER.
(At the *Great Westminster Horse Show*.)

C.-B. "NOW THEN, ORBY, OVER WE GO. I'VE TAKEN DOWN THE TOP HALF-DOZEN BARS!"
Prize Cart-Horse. "TAKE DOWN ANOTHER HALF-DOZEN, GUV'NOR, AND I'LL LOOK AT IT. BUT I'M REALLY BEST ON THE FLAT!"

Personally I am a great believer in bed, in constantly keeping horizontal ... the heart and everything go slower and the whole system is refreshed.

> SIR HENRY CAMPBELL-BANNERMAN (1836–1908)
> British Prime Minister
> 1906

On March 25, 1576, when she was ten years old, Caterina received her first communion and the same year she made a vow of virginity and perpetual

47

chastity, which rather suggests that she must have been a remarkably precocious child and withal a somewhat unpleasant one.

> E. J. DINGWALL
> *Very Peculiar People*
> 1950
> describing St Mary Magdalene de'Pazzi (1566–1607)

Poverty and eccentricity are very bad bedfellows.

> HENRY JAMES BYRON (1834–84)
> *Mirth*

A spruce little man in a doublet of green
Perambulates daily the streets and the Steyne.
Green striped is his waistcoat, his small-clothes are
    green,
And oft round his neck a green 'kerchief is seen.
Green watch-string, green seals, and, for certain,
    I've heard,
(Tho' they're powdered) green whiskers, and eke a
    green beard.
Green garters, green hose, and, deny it who can,
The brains, too, are green, of this green little man!

> 'QUIZ' on HENRY COPE
> an anonymous contributor to the *Lewes and Brighthelmstone Journal* in 1806, describing the renowned attire of Henry Cope, the most eccentrically dressed man in Brighton

I never saw a Purple Cow
I never hope to see one;
But I can tell you, anyhow,
I'd rather see than be one.
    FRANK GELETT BURGESS (1866–1951),
    US humorous writer
    The Purple Cow

Eccentricity is developed monomania.
    BAYARD TAYLOR (1825–78)
    Views A-foot
    1846

Americans are too sympathetic to provide a good milieu for the development of individuality.
    VAN WYCK BROOKS
    From a Writer's Notebook
    1957

This Isle is a mere bedlam, and therein
We all lye raving, mad in every sinne.
    MICHAEL DRAYTON (1563–1631)
    Elegy, to my Noble Friend Master William Browne
    1613

When we reached Cheesewring, our guide first led us to the house of Daniel Gumb (a stone–cutter), cut by him out of a solid rock of granite. This artificial cavern may be about twelve feet deep and not quite so broad; the roof consists of one flat stone of many tons weight; supported by the natural rock on one side, and by pillars of small stones on the other ... I have no hesitation in saying he must have been a pretty eccentric character to have fixed on this place for his habitation.

> BOND
> *Topographical and Historical Sketches of the Boroughs of East and West Looe*
> 1873

Kinquering Congs their titles take.

> WILLIAM ARCHIBALD SPOONER (1844–1930), Warden of New College, Oxford
> announcing the hymn in New College Chapel in 1879

Read every day something no-one else is reading. Think every day something no-one else is thinking. It is bad for the mind to be always a part of a unanimity.

> CHRISTOPHER MORLEY

Madam, I have been looking for a person who disliked gravy all my life; let us swear eternal friendship.

> THE REVEREND SYDNEY SMITH (1771–1845)
> *Memoir* by Lady Holland
> 1855

Cats and monkeys, monkeys and cats – all human life is there.

> HENRY JAMES (1843–1916)
> *The Madonna of the Future*

We came in early in the afternoon and while I was in the courtyard I saw a flat basket stand upon the ground the bottom of which was covered with boiled spinach. As my dog and several others in the yard had often put their noses into it I concluded it was put down for their food, not mine, till I saw a dirty girl patting it into two round balls and two children playing with it, one of whom, to lose no time, was performing an office that none could do for her. I asked the maid what she was about and what it was she was so preparing. She told me it was spinach. 'Not for me I hope,' said I. 'Oui, pour vous et le monde.' I then forbade her bringing any to table and put the little girl off her centre by an angry push ... Nevertheless, with my entree, came up a dish of this delicate spinach, with which I made the girl a very pretty Chapeau Anglais, for I turned it, dish and all upon her head.

> PHILIP THICKNESSE (1719–92), traveller
> *A Year's Journey Through France and Part of Spain*
> 1777

I must ask anyone entering the house never to contradict me in any way, as it interferes with the functioning of my gastric juices and prevents my sleeping at night.

SIR GEORGE SITWELL (1860–1943)
This message was shown on a sign in Sir
George's Derbyshire manor-house

Thanks to the march of civilisation, privacy has been exploded among us, and individuality effaced. People feel in thousands, and think in tens of thousands. No quiet nook of earth remaining for the modern Cincinnatus to cultivate his own carrots and opinions, where humours may expand into excrescence, or originality let grow its beard.

CATHERINE GORE (1799–1861)
Self

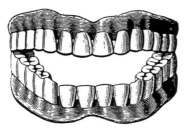

The husband was a teetotaller, there was no other woman, and the conduct complained of was that he had drifted into the habit of winding up every meal by taking out his false teeth and hurling them at his wife.

SIR ARTHUR CONAN DOYLE (1859–1930)
The Boscombe Valley Mystery

How glorious it is – and also how painful – to be an exception.

ALFRED DE MUSSET (1810–57)
The White Blackbird

I am a great and sublime fool. But then I am God's fool, and all His works must be contemplated with respect.

MARK TWAIN (1835–1910)
letter to William Dean Howells (1837–1920), 1877

Mrs Nott told me that Louie of the Cloggau was staying in Presteign with her aunt Miss Sylvester, the woman frog. This extraordinary being is partly a woman and partly a frog. Her head and face, her eyes and mouth are those of a frog, and she has frog's legs and feet. She cannot walk but she hops ... She is a very good person.

THE REVEREND FRANCIS KILVERT (1840–79)
Diary

And as the feeling of being a stranger and an exile by nature as well as by accident grew upon me in time, it came to be almost a point of pride; some people may have thought it an affectation. It was not that. I have always admired the normal child of his age and country.

> GEORGE SANTAYANA (1863–1952)
> in *Atlantic Monthly*, January 1949

I dislike monkeys: they always remind me of poor relations.

> HENRY LUTTRELL (1770–1851)quoted in *Familiar Short Sayings of Great Men* by SAMUEL A. BENT, 1887

There was an old man of Thermopylae
Who never did anything properly;
But they said, 'If you choose
To boil eggs in your shoes,
Your shall never remain in Thermopylae.'
> EDWARD LEAR (1812–88)
> *One Hundred Nonsense Pictures and Rhymes*

Jean Baptiste du Val de Grace Clootz (1755–94) … while still young traversed Europe under the name of Anarcharsis, lavishing his money to promote the union of all nations in one family. In the French Revolution he saw the fulfilment of his dreams. He constituted himself the 'orator of the human race', and wearied the National Assembly with his ravings against Christianity. With all its folly his enthusiasm was honest.

> CHAMBERS' *BIOGRAPHICAL DICTIONARY*
> 1898

Eccentricity exists particularly in the English, and partly, I think, because of that peculiar and satisfactory knowledge of infallibility that is the hallmark and birthright of the British nation.

> EDITH SITWELL (1887–1964)
> *The English Eccentrics*
> 1933

The perfection of several of the preparations is so exquisitely evanescent that the delay of one minute after their arrival at the meridian of concoction will render them no longer worthy of men of taste.

> DR WILLIAM KITCHINER, nineteenth-century founder and secretary of the Eta Beta Pi dining club on his policy of refusing entrance to late arrivals to his dinners

What a damned slow fellow you must have been all your life!

> JOHN MYTTON (1796–1834)
> in response to a friend who remarked that he had never been overturned in a gig before. Mytton, a countryside sporting eccentric, often hunted naked, and once arrived at a dinner party riding a brown bear

The trick of singularity.

> WILLIAM SHAKESPEARE (1564–1616)
> *Twelfth Night*

My only fear is, that I may be deficient in strength of pencil to draw the picture to the life, and to represent the anomaly in human nature which the character of John Mytton presents ... The barber's shop was now and then the scene of a 'lark'. Entering it one evening, Mytton asked what he could have to drink? but, before an answer could be given him, he snatched up a bottle of lavender-water, and, knocking off the head of it, drank it off at a draught, saying, 'It was a good preservative against the bad effects of night air.'

C. J. APPERLEY
Memoirs of the Life of the Late John Mytton, Esq
1871

He is a beautiful and ineffectual angel beating in the void his luminous wings in vain.

MATTHEW ARNOLD (1822–88)
Essays in Criticism: 'Shelley'

He had a routine. He'd walk through the house every morning before he left, open the door of each room with a key, peer in, then relock it. Then at night when he came home he would unlock each door, turn the light on, lock up, and go to bed.

JED JOHNSON on ANDY WARHOL (1928–87)
in *The Andy Warhol Collection Catalogues*

The obedient well-behaved citizen who does his duty is not a 'hero'. Only an individual who has fashioned his 'self-will', his noble, natural inner law, into his destiny can be a hero.

HERMANN HESSE (1877–1962)
If the War Goes On

Mr Damer made [Adam Smith, 1723–90] a visit the other morning as he was going to breakfast, and falling into discourse, Mr Smith took a piece of bread and butter, which after he had rolled round and round, he put into the teapot; and, when he had tasted it, he said it was the worst tea he had ever met with.

JOHN RAE
Life of Adam Smith
1895

No society in which eccentricity is a matter of reproach, can be in a wholesome state.

J. S. MILL (1802–73)
On Liberty
1859

A noble nasty course he ran
Superbly filthy and fastidious,
He was the world's first gentleman
And made that appellation hideous.
WINTHROP MACKWORTH PRAED (1802–39)
Poems, 1864
on King George IV

You have expressed a desire to know what led me to assume male attire. I will try to tell you. I think I was born into this world with some dormant antagonism towards man. I hope I have outgrown it measurably but my infant soul was impressed with a sense of my mother's wrongs before I ever saw the light and I probably drew from her breast with my daily food my love of independence and my hatred of male tyranny.
SARAH EMMA EDMONDS, the most famous female soldier of the American Civil War
quoted in *Post and Tribune* by Frank Schneider, 1883

Lawrence, an odd gnome, half cad – with a touch of genius.
THE HON. AUBREY HERBERT on T.E. LAWRENCE (1888–1935)
note in private diary, 1914

To burn always with this hard, gemlike flame, to maintain this ecstasy, is success in life.

> WALTER PATER (1839–94)
> *Studies in the History of the Renaissance*
> 1873

Well, I must say that the first man who threw peas at me was a publican, while I was giving an entertainment to a few of my admirers in a public-house in a certain little village not far from Dundee; but my dear friends, I wish it to be understood that the publican who threw the peas at me was not the landlord of the public-house, he was one of the party who came to hear me give my entertainment.

> WILLIAM McGONAGALL (1830–1902), poet
> *Reminiscences*
> 1890

So long as a man rides his hobby-horse peaceably and quietly along the King's highway, and neither compels you or me to get up behind him, – pray, Sir, what have either you or I to do with it?

> LAURENCE STERNE (1713–68)
> *Tristram Shandy*
> 1759–67

There's Bardus, a six-foot column of fop,
A lighthouse without any light atop.

> THOMAS HOOD (1799–1845)
> *Miss Kilmansegg*

I look in the glass sometimes at my two long, cylindrical bags (so picturesquely rugged about the knees), my stand-up collar and billycock hat, and wonder what right I have to go about making God's world hideous ... I want to put on lavender-coloured tights, with red velvet breeches and a green doublet, slashed with yellow ... Let me be a butterfly.

> JEROME K. JEROME (1859–1927)
> *Idle Thoughts of an Idle Fellow*
> 1889

No member of a crew is praised for the rugged individuality of his rowing.

> RALPH WALDO EMERSON (1803–82)
> *Essays*

If, this gay favourite lost, they yet can live,
A tear to Selwyn let the Graces give!
With rapid kindness teach oblivion's pall
O'er the sunk foibles of the man to fall;
And fondly dictate to a faithful Muse
The prime distinction of the friend they lose.
'Twas social wit, which, never kindling strife,
Blazed in the small, sweet courtesies of life;
Those little sapphires round the diamond shone,
Lending soft radiance to the richer stone.
     anonymous epitaph for GEORGE AUGUSTUS
     SELWYN (1719–91), society wit
     quoted in *Wits, Beaux and Beauties of the
     Georgian Era* by John Fyvie, 1909

When I'm playful I use the meridians of longitude and
parallels of latitude for a seine [net], and drag the
Atlantic Ocean for whales. I scratch my head with

the lightning and purr myself to sleep with the thunder.

> MARK TWAIN (1835–1910)
> *Life on the Mississippi*
> 1883

It is perfectly easy to be original by violating the laws of decency and the canons of good taste.

> OLIVER WENDELL HOLMES, SEN. (1809–94)
> *Over The Teacups*
> 1891

Why not be one's self? That is the whole secret of a successful appearance. If one is a greyhound, why try to look like a Pekingese? ... I am as highly stylised as it

is possible to be – as stylised as the music of Debussy or
Ravel.

> EDITH SITWELL (1887–1964)
> 'Why I Look The Way I Do' in the *Sunday
> Graphic*, 4 December 1955

Once we all call a man a 'crank', it is certain that we
are prepared to dislike him, whereas, unless we are
raging pretorians of convention, we feel a sort of
tenderness for the eccentric.

> J. B. PRIESTLEY (1894–1984)
> All About Ourselves and Other Essays

John Grubby, who was short and stout
And troubled with religious doubt,
Refused about the age of three
To sit upon the curate's knee.

> G. K. CHESTERTON (1874–1936)
> *The New Freethinker*

We might define an eccentric as a man who is a law
unto himself, and a crank as one who, having
determined what the law is, insists on laying it down
to others.

> LOUIS KRONENBERGER
> *Company Manners*
> 1954

There was something about him, the proud man apart, the Don Quixote on a bicycle.

> PAUL POTTS on GEORGE ORWELL (1903–50)
> in the *London Magazine*, March 1957

Woe to every mortal, and especially in these days, who affects singularity in order to be a personage.

> VOLTAIRE (1694–1778)
> *Vanity*

Charles Domery ('The Remarkable Glutton') … was one of nine brothers who, with their father, were remarkable for the voraciousness of their appetites … When in the [army] camp, if bread or meat were scarce, he made up the deficiency by eating four or five pounds of grass daily; and in one year devoured 174 cats (not their skins) dead or alive … Dogs and rats equally suffered from his merciless jaws.

> HENRY WILSON AND JAMES CAULFIELD
> *The Book of Wonderful Characters*
> 1869

He that will keep a monkey should pay for the glass he breaks.

> JOHN SELDEN (1584–1654)
> *Table Talk*
> 1689

t is universally admitted that no country in the world
produces so many humorists and eccentric characters
as the British islands. This acknowledgment is an
indirect eulogy on the political constitution and the
laws under which the English enjoy the happiness of
living, and by which each individual is suffered to
gratify every whim, fancy, and caprice, provided it be
not prejudicial to his fellow creatures.

>   HENRY WILSON
>   *The Eccentric Mirror*
>   1813

want to be unobtrusive.

>   HOWARD HUGHES (1905–76)
>   on himself, in an interview with United Press
>   International

Who's your fat friend?
> BEAU BRUMMELL (1778–1840)
> on the Prince of Wales

I declare that the earth is hollow, habitable within ...
I pledge my life in support of this truth, and am ready
to explore the hollow if the world will support and aid
me in the undertaking.
> JOHN CLEEVES SYMMES (1780–1829)
> quoted in *The Square Pegs* by Irving Wallace,
> 1958
> Symmes's campaign led in 1823 to the future
> Vice-President of the USA, Richard Johnson,
> requesting Congress to fund the exploration

Men will always be mad and those who think they can
cure them are the maddest of all.
> VOLTAIRE (1694–1778)
> letter, 1762

If I treat my body properly, I believe I'll live to 150.
> MICHAEL JACKSON (1957–), singer

Barbara Villiers, Duchess of Cleveland (1640–1709)
deserves to be placed very near the worst of the bad
women of history ... She was a bad wife, a bad
mother, and a worse mistress. She was inordinately
avaricious and madly extravagant. She gambled and
she swore, and she had neither wit nor sense, and

never did an unselfish thing. She had the temper of a fiend and the manners of a fishwife.

> *Lives of twelve bad women – illustrations and reviews of feminine turpitude set forth by impartial hands*
> edited by Arthur Vincent
> 1847

The art of life is to be thought odd. Everything will then be permitted to you. The best way to be thought odd is to return a cheque now and then on a conscientious scruple.

> E. V. LUCAS (1868–1938)
> *365 Days and One More*

Cauliflower is nothing but cabbage with a college education.

> MARK TWAIN (1835–1910)
> *Pudd'nhead Wilson's Character*

She possessed extraordinary powers of conversation, and was perfectly fascinating to all with whom she chose to make herself agreeable. She was, however, whimsical, imperious, tyrannical and at times, revengeful to a degree. Bold as a lion, she wore the dress of an Emir, weapons, pipe and all ... She was wholly and magnificently unique.

> THE REVEREND W.M. THOMPSON on LADY HESTER
> STANHOPE (1776–1839), traveller
> *The Land and the Book*
> 1898

I caught a cat and having administered a large dose of arsenic, I chloroformed it, hanged it above the gas jet, stabbed it, cut its throat, smashed its skull, and when it had been pretty thoroughly burnt, drowned it and threw it out of the window that the fall might remove the ninth life. The operation was successful. I was genuinely sorry for the animal; I simply forced myself to carry out the experiment in the interests of pure science.

> ALEISTER CROWLEY (1875–1947)
> *The Spirit of Solitude: An Autohagiography*
> Crowley claimed he was attempting to prove
> that a cat had nine lives

Tread where the traffic does not go.

> CALLIMANCHUS (c. 310–246 BC)
> *Fragments*

I am neither of a melancholy nor a cynical disposition, and am as willing and as apt to be pleased as anybody; but I am sure that, since I have had the full use of my reason, nobody has ever heard me laugh.

> PHILIP DARMER STANHOPE, EARL OF CHESTERFIELD
> (1694–1773)
> in a letter to his son
> 9 March 1748

Men and women one of these days will have the courage to be eccentric. They will do as they like – just as the great ones have always done. The word eccentric is a term of reproach and mild contempt and amusement today, because we live under a system which hates real originality.

> HOLBROOK JACKSON
> *Southward Ho! and Other Essays*

Force is all that matters. War is sacred. Hanging is excellent. We don't need too much knowledge. Build more prisons and fewer schools.

> VICTOR HUGO (1802–85)
> *The Terrible Years*
> 1872

Of the parsimoniousness of Mrs Sobieski Killingbecks [who lived in London in the late eighteenth century], there was no question. She dreaded to see the consumption of any necessary thing in her house, no matter what might be its nature, nor how customary and needful it might be in housekeeping. Soap was a forbidden expense, as soft water would do as well, except for the little washing which she needed, and performed herself as was remarked by an old lady in a tobacco shop, who knew something of her ways, and was now and then permitted to visit her ... She used to talk of Frederick the Great of Prussia, as if she had seen him, but did not highly commend him.

> CYRUS REDDING
> *Memoirs of Remarkable Misers*
> 1863

Van Butchell, not wishing to be unpleasantly circumstanced, and wishing to convince some good minds they have been misinformed, acquaints the Curious, no stranger can see his embalmed wife unless (by a friend personally) introduced by himself, any day between nine and one, Sundays excepted.

> MARTIN VAN BUTCHELL
> advertisement placed in the *St James's Chronicle*,
> 31 October 1875, by Martin Van Butchell, who
> so missed his deceased wife that he kept her,
> embalmed, on show in his front room

He [Alexander Cruden, 1701–70] was a philanthropist and a missionary, an egoist and an enthusiast. He was a true Eccentric, for his ways were not concentric with the circles among which he moved: throughout his life he followed his own orbit.

EDITH OLIVER
The Eccentric Life of Alexander Cruden
1934

All strangeness and self-particularity in our manners and conditions is to be shunned as an enemy to society and civil conversation.

MICHEL EYQUEM DE MONTAIGNE (1533–92)
Essays I. XXV
1580

He [Richard Nash, 1674–1762] was naturally endued with good sense; but by having been long accustomed to pursue trifles, his mind shrunk to the size of the little objects on which it was employed ... He chose to be thought rather an odd fellow, than a well-loved man; perhaps that mixture of respect and ridicule, with which his mock royalty was treated, first inspired him with this resolution.

OLIVER GOLDSMITH (1730–74)
The Life of Richard Nash of Bath
1762
Richard Nash, 'Beau Nash', was master of ceremonies at Bath, where he conducted the public balls and took an imperial influence with fashionable society

In the year 1908 one of the largest meteorites the world has ever known was hurled at the earth. It missed its mark. It hit Siberia. I was born in Sutton, in Surrey.

As soon as I stepped out of my mother's womb on to dry land, I realised I had made a mistake – that I shouldn't have come.

QUENTIN CRISP
The Naked Civil Servant
1968

When he [W.H. Auden] stayed with the Carritts, he removed their stair-carpet, still in search of nocturnal warmth, and placed it on the bed. He always got on well with Mrs Carritt, even though at breakfast on the first morning, he tasted his tea and then said flatly, 'Mrs Carritt, this tea is like tepid piss.'

CHARLES OSBORNE
W. H. Auden: The Life of a Poet
1980

If a patient is poor, he is committed to a public hospital as 'psychotic'; if he can afford the luxury of a private sanitarium, he is put there with the diagnosis of 'neurasthenia'; if he is wealthy enough to be isolated in his own home under constant watch of nurses and physicians he is simply an indisposed 'eccentric'.

> PIERRE MARIE FELIX JARRET (1859–1947), French
> psychologist
> *La Force et la faiblesse psychologiques*

She [Catherine Hyde, Duchess of Queensberry] was, in reality, insane, though the politeness of fashionable society, and the flattery of her poetical friends, seem rather to have attributed her extravagances to an agreeable freedom of carriage and vivacity of mind. When she went out to an evening entertainment, and found a tea-equipage paraded which she thought too fine for the rank of the owner, she would contrive to overset the table, and break the china. The forced politeness of her hosts on such occasions, and the assurances which they made her Grace that no harm was done, delighted her exceedingly.

> ROBERT CHAMBERS
> *Traditions of Edinburgh*
> 1825

If a man does not keep pace with his companions, perhaps it is because he hears a different drummer. Let him step to the music which he hears, however measured or far away.

> HENRY DAVID THOREAU (1817–62)
> *Walden*
> 1854

Whatever became of old Shelley?
Is it true that young Briggs was cashiered
For riding quite nude on a pushbike through Delhi
The day the new Viceroy appeared?
    NOEL COWARD (1899–1973)
    I Wonder What Happened To Him?
    from *Sigh No More*, 1945

One hair of a woman can draw more than a hundred pair of oxen.
    JAMES HOWELL (1594–1666)
    Familiar Letters

Tree-hugging was invented by Rod Nicholson, a former headmaster who runs the Centre for Harmony in Gloucester ... Mr Nicholson holds special seven-hour, tree-healing courses over the weekend. Apparently there's more to hugging a tree than meets the eye – the right breathing technique and posture are essential to connect with its 'stillness, strength and centredness' ... Mr Nicholson, 53, denies that treehugging is an eccentric activity: 'People in Britain are already very in touch with nature.'
    report in the *Independent* newspaper, 13
    September 1993

I have all my life been seeking for a butcher whose respect for genius predominated over his love of gain ... The other day [my butcher] called and I had him sent up into the painting-room. I found him in great admiration of *Alexander*. 'Quite alive, sir!' 'I am glad you think so,' said I. 'Yes, sir; but as I have said often to my sister, you could not have painted that picture, sir, if you had not eat my meat, sir!' 'Very true, Mr Sowerby.' 'Ah! sir I have a fancy for *genius*, sir!'

> BENJAMIN HAYDON (1786–1846), painter
> in a letter to Mary Russell Mitford (1787–1855)
> 1826

Dante – known to [Mr Sparkler] as an eccentric man in the nature of an Old File, who used to put leaves round his head, and sit upon a stool for some unaccountable purpose, outside the cathedral in Florence.

> CHARLES DICKENS (1812–70)
> *Little Dorrit*
> 1855

Thank God for eccentrics! Take Gunner Octavian Neat. He would suddenly appear naked in a barrack room and say, 'Does anybody know a good tailor?' or 'Gentlemen – I think there's a thief in the battery.'

> SPIKE MILLIGAN (1919–)
> Adolf Hitler: My Part in his Downfall
> 1971

I guess I'm just an old mad scientist at bottom. Give me an underground laboratory, half a dozen atom-smashers, and a beautiful girl in a diaphanous veil waiting to be turned into a chimpanzee, and I care not who writes the nation's laws.

> S. J. PERELMAN (1904–79)
> Captain Future, Block That Kick!
> from *The Most of S. J. Perelman*
> 1978

Who would have supposed that from a man who was absolutely a fop, finikin in dress, with mincing steps and tremulous words, with his hair curled and full of unguents, and his cheeks painted like those of frivolous demirep, would flame out ultimately the depravity of a poisoner and a murderer?

> THOMAS SECCOMBE
> *Lives of Twelve Bad Men*
> 1894
> describing Thomas Griffiths Wainewright,
> 1794–1852, the infamous poisoner who ended
> up awaiting execution in prison tormenting his
> fellow-prisoners with tales of hell

A man who would be a man must be a non-conformist; he must hold Plato at arm's length, say to him, 'You have been pleasing the world for two thousand years, see whether you can please me.'

> SILAS BENT
> *Life of Oliver Wendell Holmes*
> quoting Ralph Waldo Emerson (1803–82)

William McClellan, Lord Kirkudbright, father of John, seventh Lord, whose right was confirmed by a decision of the House of Lords, in 1773, followed the occupation of a glover, in Edinburgh, and, for many years, used to stand in the lobby of the Assembly-rooms in the Old Town, selling gloves to gentlemen, who, according to the fashionable etiquette of the period, required a new pair at every new dance. His Lordship never absented himself from his post upon any occasion, excepting at the ball which followed the election of a representative peer, and then, and then only, did he assume the badge of a gentleman, and, doffing his apron, become one of a company, the most of whom he usually served with his merchandize all the rest of the year.

> J. BERNARD BURKE
> *Anecdotes of the Aristocracy*
> 1849

Thou star with a tail, thou eccentric man.

> THE AMIR OF BUKHARA, Central Asia, to DR JOSEPH
> WOLFF (1795–1862)
> in *A Mission to Bukhara* by Joseph Wolff

On more than one occasion, having departed to bed with the *Bhagavad Gita* or *The Cloud of Unknowing* prominently displayed beneath her arm, I subsequently discovered her, when I went to say good-night, deep in the latest work of Miss Ethel M. Dell. Always on such occasions her response, uttered in a very reproachful tone, to any expression of surprise was the same, 'You know quite well, dear, that the bent bow must be unstrung.'

> OSBERT LANCASTER
> *With An Eye To The Future*
> 1967
> on his mother

When someone asked him later why he had not involved the public more in the question of Vietnam, he was told, 'If you have a mother-in-law with only one eye and she has it in the centre of her forehead, you don't keep her in the living-room.'

> LYNDON BAINES JOHNSON (1908–73)
> quoted in *The Best and the Brightest*, by D. Halberstram, 1972

The Marquis of Blandford was of no great depth: apt to great fits of laughter at trifles. On Mr Richardson's filliping a piece of bread into the blind fiddler's face, it held him for half an hour, and returned whenever the thing was only mentioned afterwards.

> JOSEPH SPENCE (1699–1768)
> *Observations, Anecdotes, and Characters of Books and Men*
> 1820
> quoting Jonathan Richardson (1694–1771)

There is not a man of the nation, no, not even Lord Effingham, who bestows so much time and attempts in rendering the external appearance of his head, elegant in the extreme, than the Earl of Scarborough. It is said that his Lordship keeps six French friseurs, who have nothing else to do than dress his hair. Lord Effingham keeps only five.

    Morning Post, 4 July 1789

The world *does* move, and its motive power under God is the fearless thought and speech of those who dare to be in advance of their time – who are sneered at and shunned through their days of struggle as lunatics, dreamers, impracticables and visionaries; men of crotchets, vagaries, and isms. They are the masts and sails of the ship to which conservatism answers as ballast.

    HORACE GREELEY (1811–72), American writer
    New York Tribune
    1845

Take the case of the Slaves on American plantations. I dare say they are worked hard, I dare say they don't altogether like it, I dare say theirs is an unpleasant experience on the whole; but they people the landscape for me, they give it a poetry for me, and perhaps that is one of the pleasanter objects of their existence. I am very sensible of it, if it be, and I shouldn't wonder if it were!

> CHARLES DICKENS (1812–70)
> *Bleak House*
> 1852

Scotland ... is the home of the world's largest pineapple, built in 1791. The pineapple is 40 feet tall, made of concrete, and it perches atop the 50-foot central tower of Dunmore Castle in Stirlingshire. It has to be noted, however, that the eccentric Earl of Dunmore, who built the massive fruit, eventually emigrated to the United States.

> J. J. C. ANDREWS
> *The Well-Built Elephant: A Tribute to American Eccentricity*
> 1984

'B.M.' [Lady Sackville] fascinated me, for many of her qualities were opposed by a wholly contradictory set of qualities. At one moment she was a great lady, mistress of Knole and a friend of kings; a few moments later a peasant, giving one morsels of food in her fingers from her plate and saying, 'Eat this, eat this, it is so good.' Though in many ways she was madly extravagant, in others she was eccentrically mean.

> CHRISTABEL ABERCONWAY (1890–1974)
> *A Wiser Woman?*

Madame Dieulafoy always dressed as a man and wore men's clothes whenever she went abroad to attend to her multitudinous occupations; But Madame Dieulafoy, who thus put on the man, had some strange ideas of her own. She maintained that feminine education, that is, educating all children as girls, was the only way of teaching young folk to behave properly in society. Quite seriously, Madame Dieulafoy confidently hoped that these boys in shirts and petticoats, simpering, ogling and toying with their fans, would make nineteenth century France as polished and well-behaved as France of the eighteenth century had been: a strange notion, defensible only because there is something to be said for almost everything.

OSCAR GILBERT
Women in Men's Guise
1932

Miss Blanchford is agreeable enough. I do not want people to be very agreeable, as it saves me the trouble of liking them a great deal.

JANE AUSTEN (1775–1817)
Letters
24 December 1798

It is now eleven years since I have seen my figure in a glass, and the last reflection I saw there was so

disagreeable that I resolved to spare myself the
mortification in the future.

> MARY WORTLEY MONTAGU (1689–1762)
> *Letters of the Right Honourable Lady Mary Wortley
> Montagu*
> 1767

Alexander asked him if he lacked anything. 'Yes,' he
said, 'that I do: that you stand out of my sun a little.'

> PLUTARCH (46–120)
> *Life of Alexander*
> on the cynic philosopher Diogenes (412–323
> BC), who was said to have lived in a bath

There's no getting blood out of a turnip.

> FREDERICK MARRYAT (1792–1848)
> *Japhet in Search of a Father*
> 1836

So many people have told me that they enjoy reading
my books tremendously and how much happiness I
have brought into their marriages that I wondered
how I could be even more helpful to those who need
me.

> DAME BARBARA CARTLAND
> in the *Independent* newspaper, 9 October 1993,
> launching her own Romance Club

She's as headstrong as an allegory on the banks of the Nile.

    RICHARD BRINSLEY SHERIDAN (1751–1816)
    The Rivals
    1775

When [Timothy Dwight, 1752–1817] came to be a tutor at [Yale University] his demands upon himself grew still more strict. Covetous of time, he determined to avoid all waste of it through so base a thing as bodily exercise, by extinguishing the need of bodily exercise; and this he expected to accomplish by gradually lessening the quantity of his food. His success was very striking. He so far reduced his diet that he was able to dine on just twelve mouthfuls. That, of course, was his most luxurious meal; but for breakfast and supper he deemed it his duty to be less abandoned to gluttony.

    MOSES COIT TYLER
    Three Men of Letters
    1895

How rarely I meet with a man who can be free, even in thought! We all live according to rule. Some men are bed-ridden; all are worldridden.

    HENRY DAVID THOREAU (1817–62)
    The Heart of Thoreau's Journal
    edited by Odell Shepard
    1839

My only great qualification for being in charge of the
Navy is that I am very much at sea.

SIR EDWARD CARSON (1854–1935)
on himself quoted in *Carson* by H. Montgomery
Hyde, 1953